He's the Master of Every Situation

The Life and Faith of Mother Boyd

Writings of Mother Boyd
and Testimonies Submitted by
Otis Boyd

Revised and Compiled by
Timothy M. Harris, II

Editing by
Jennifer E. Clark
Timothy M. Harris

Just Word Publishing, LLC
Indianapolis, IN

He's the Master of Every Situation
Revised and Updated Edition

Published by
Just Word Publishing, LLC
4501 N. Post Rd.
Indianapolis, IN 46226-4130
www.justwordministries.com

All scripture quotations are from King James Version of the Bible.

Design & layout by:
Timothy M. Harris, II
Timothy M. Harris
Angela M. Rogers

Graphics by Angela M. Rogers

Printed in the United States of America.

ISBN: 978-0-97713-130-3

Contents

Foreword by Pastor Timothy M. Harris

Section 1
My Personal Testimony

Section 2
Healings of Others

Section 3

Deliverance & More

Section 4

In Loving Memory of Mother

Section 5

Index

The Word of God is demanding. It demands a stretch of time in our day – even though the length may be a very modest one – in which the Word is our only companion. God will not put up with being fobbed off with prayers in telegram style and cut short like a troublesome visitor for whom we open the door just a crack to get rid of him as quickly as possible.

Foreword

This book is in loving memory of my friend Mildred Boyd, who I affectionately and respectfully knew as "Mother." She was one of the greatest faith healers of our time, and any time since the creation of mankind, and her healing and prophetic ministry greatly impacted my life and the life of thousands of others. Through her ministry, friends and family members were healed and most importantly saved.

My son Timmy II ("Two") received healing of seizures in 1990, at the age of ten. I remember this miracle like it was yesterday. Mother Boyd said to me, "It's time son. Get your son and bring him into the Young People's room so we can pray for him. God said, 'He's going to heal your son.'" In typical Mother Boyd fashion, she prayed a prayer that was very short: "God, in the name of Jesus Christ, we need your help! Heal, like I know You're able!" Immediately after the prayer, she told me, "God said, 'He's going to have one more. It will be the worst one he's ever had.' But don't worry son, the work is done. He'll never have another one after that."

The next morning, Two woke up screaming, "Dad!" After dashing into his room, he said, "My leg!" This was how it always started. His leg was shaking out of control. Then his whole body began shaking, though he was stiff as a board. His little brown eyes rolled in the back of his head and he lost all control of his bodily functions. There I sat holding my son, reminding myself and thanking God that this was the last one he'd ever have.

Though he had seizures since he was about three months old that increased in their frequency and intensity as he got older, though the neurologist diagnosed him as having an inherited genetic disorder, though the EEG showed abnormal brain activity, and though neither Tegritol nor any medicine was helpful in the treatment, still God healed him! Two is now grown, and just like God said (without any medication or physician involvement), he has not had another seizure since.

Mother Boyd also impacted me personally. I remember having a job offer in my pocket that would have paid me $300,000 per year, minimum. I had planned to ask her to pray whether it was God's will for me to accept this job, but on the way home, before I could utter a word, she told me to pull over into a school parking lot so we could pray. Before God revealed it to her, she had no idea that I had an offer. Again she prayed a short prayer for God to bless me, then said, "God said, 'Don't take the offer! Start your own business!'" Then she prayed again that the Lord give me favor with the customers and gave me another word about Psalm 70 being mine and that I should pray it. Long story short, Harris & Ford, LLC sales were $1.8 million our first year in business, and grew to about $250 million annually. When people ask why I started my business and how it's been so successful, my response amazes them when I start off by saying, "Well, there was this older lady I took to a restaurant, I called her Mother Boyd..."

Until we meet in Heaven, I will forever miss the times we shared – eating out, going for rides after service, and mostly, joining hands, hearts, and minds in prayer. This book is my way of telling God, Mother Boyd, and her son Otis that was raised from the dead, "Thank You!"

Timothy M. Harris
Just Word Ministries
www.justwordministries.com

Section 1

My Personal Testimony

Mother Boyd before God healed her eye of cancer and gave her 20/20 vision in both eyes.

Autobiography of Mildred Boyd

I was born in Fredonia, Kentucky at my grandfather's house; his name was Andy Stone. He was a businessman. My parents, Herman and Bessie Crider, had his first grandchild. On the day I was born, my grandfather went to the bank, took money out of his account, and put it in another account under my name so I could go to school. He taught me I could have anything that money could buy. We did not have charge cards in those days. But I could go into any store and say I was Andy Stone's granddaughter, and I was able to buy whatever I wanted. My grandfather also taught me about being a lady, and I went by his rules and regulations. I was brought up in a very strict home.

At the age of twelve, I was converted in the CME Methodist Church. At the age of thirteen, the church members discovered that I had unusual abilities. They made up in their minds that they were going to train me to be a great leader in the CME Church. They sent me to school in many cities, such as: Washington, D.C.; Perkiomenville, PA; Toledo, Cleveland, and Cincinnati, Ohio. They sent me to those cities thinking I would be a great teacher in the CME Church. God blessed me for just that work.

Three men in Mother Boyd's life; Herman Crider, father; Hugh Boyd, husband; and Otis Boyd, son.

When I grew up, I married Hugh Boyd and had a very happy home. God blessed me with a son, Otis, and we also adopted a daughter, Martha Ann.

Then one day I went to the Jesus-only church. I would go on Sunday night when our church was over; listening to the testimonies of what the mighty God was able to do. I did not enjoy the preaching at first, so I would get up and leave before the preaching started. But one night I sat there too long, and the preacher got up and began to preach. My training was not to move once the preacher stood up. When I heard the word of God, I was convinced that I was not saved according to the word of God. I repented of my sins and was baptized during the young people's service. Elder Hall at Christ Temple baptized me, and God filled me with the Holy Ghost. The scales fell from my eyes, and I knew that I had the Bible salvation.

My husband did not get saved right away. He did not understand, but he watched my life. Finally, one Wednesday night before Thanksgiving, he made up his mind that "whatever my wife has, I've got to have it." He went to church and told God, "I have to have it tonight. If they close the church, I'll be there tomorrow, because I don't have to work Thanksgiving Day." In less than fifteen minutes, God filled him with the Holy Ghost. We lived a beautiful life together.

God called me into the ministry. I was blessed to study Old Testament under Dr. Nockorhy at Butler University and the New Testament at Indiana University. I thank and praise God that He opened up my understanding to His word that I might be able to help others who were in church darkness such as I was.

I was taught faith. I was taught that it is impossible to please God without faith. Christ Temple had faith and healing night every Thursday night. They prayed for the sick and taught us faith.

I was sick when I was young. I had hay fever, rose fever, asthma, and a very nervous stomach. I stayed in the doctor's office all the time. I got in the prayer line one Thursday night, was prayed for by Sister Mattie Poole from Chicago, Illinois, and God healed me of every illness I had.

I thank God for faith because seven years after my healing, I developed cancer on my right side. God spoke to me and said that it was cancer. I was actually in the last stage of cancer. I suffered so, I begged God to take me home! God said, "You can't die; you haven't been to the east (to minister) yet." God healed me and smoothed my body out without aspirin or anything.

Several years after that, I had cancer of my left eye. By faith, I believed God. The devil fought me and told me that the cancer would cross over to the other side and cause blindness. But, God healed me and gave me 20/20 vision. I know God is a healer and a keeper.

In January 1980, I had two heart attacks and a stroke the same night. I was in revival, and this happened in the church. My pastor was there, as well as a former pastor's wife. They gathered around me and laid hands on me, and God healed me of the heart attack and stroke at my church. I went home feeling fine. But, going up and down the steps, I had the second heart attack, and that time my son called Cheryl Wright, a nurse. When she came to my home and saw me, she knew I was dying and said, We're not going to lay her down. She's going so fast, and we want to keep her as long as we can."

They called all over the country to the pastors and requested prayer for me. They called Youngstown, Ohio to Dr. Norman

Wagner. He had just walked in his home. He turned around and went back to the church and prayed until day. God spoke out and told him, "I won't take her." Dr. Wagner went to the telephone and called my house and told them what God said, and he asked them to tell me. They said, "she's too far gone; she doesn't know a thing." He said, "Whisper in her ear and tell her what God said." Sister Wright whispered in my ear and told me what God said. When she did, my heart struck a normal beat, and my pulse took a normal beat. She said to the family, "We're going to lay her down; she's fallen into normal sleep." I slept until noon. She came in to bathe me and dress me and asked how I was feeling. I said, "Fine and I'm hungry." She asked me, "What do you want to eat?" I said, "Fried chicken and Pepsi Cola." She laughed and said, "It will be a long time before you get that." I just asked you to see what you were going to say. God gave me complete victory and put me back on my feet.

I can say that He's a savior, a healer, a keeper, and a mind regulator. He's everything that you ever needed Him to be.

My Husband's Heart Failure

I would like now to tell of my husband's testimony. My husband decided that we would adopt two other boys and two other girls. He always wanted a big family because he was the only child in his family. I decided that we would take welfare children at first, and then find out if we wanted to adopt. He said that we could have six children for Sunday school: three girls and three boys. Then we called the welfare people, and they came out and investigated our house. They said that they would hate to put children in a home this nice because the children could really mess up things. My husband said that we could train them. However, to qualify to be foster parents, we had to have physical examinations. We made an appointment with the doctor.

After the examinations, the doctor called my husband in first, then he called me. When I went in, my husband was still undressed. The doctor said to me, "Six months is all the time this man has to live. His heart is so large it has almost covered the whole lung. He has hardening arteries and high blood pressure. He could have a stroke before he gets out of here." He told me that he should straighten up his business because six months is as long as he has to live. "We're not going to give him any medicine because there is no medicine that will help. I don't want him to work another day."

When we walked out, my husband said, "Baby, I'm going to work and take care of my family." We called the welfare people and told them we couldn't keep the children. We fasted and prayed. God spoke out and said, "He's healed." When we testified to it, the people did not believe it. I took out a big insurance policy, the kind you pay every six months. The insurance companies examined the people they insured. When I called them and told them the kind of policy I wanted, they said, "We will have to examine him." That was what I wanted. Their doctor came out and examined him and asked him question after question. He couldn't believe that he had suffered such bad health, and yet couldn't find anything wrong with him. He had him jumping and jumping on the floor, and then he examined him again. He said, "Your blood pressure is normal, your heartbeat is perfect, and I cannot find anything wrong with you."

We took out the insurance policy, Glory to God! My husband lived to see both of his children grown and out of school. When he went home to be with the Lord, his baby was twenty-six years old. Glory to God; God is the master of every situation.

My Husband's Foot Injury

S everal years after the children were grown and on their own, my husband came home and got out of the truck. He staggered, and the two back wheels of the truck ran over his foot, crushing and mangling the bones in his foot. When he came in, he said, Call the company and tell them I won't be coming to work tomorrow." When I did, the man at the company asked what happened, and I told him. He said, "Tell your husband that he will have to go to the doctor within so many hours of the incident." My husband said to tell him that he was not going to the doctor. The man said, "If he doesn't go, he won't have a job. I said to my husband, "You could go; you don't have to take the medicine."

We went to Methodist Hospital, and the doctors x-rayed his foot. They called the bone specialist to come in and take off his foot that night. My husband said, "I didn't come here for that." The doctor said, "But there's no bone in your foot to set. It is all mangled in with the blood. We'll have to take the foot off in order to save your life." My husband said, "But I didn't come here for that." The doctor asked, "Why would you want to go home?" He said, "I have somebody I want to talk to." The doctor asked me, "What are you going to do? I said, "Whatever he says." He said, "Tomorrow will be too late to save his life. By then, his foot will be as black as the hair on his head." My husband said, "I want to go home." The doctor asked, "Will you come back tomorrow?" My husband said, "If that's what you want."

I brought him home and called the saints, those that believe God can do anything. They came and bowed on their knees and began to pray. There were three couples, and a mother with her daughter. While they were praying, my husband said, "Everything is alright. Somebody has touched the throne." They got up and shook his hand and walked out the door.

The next morning he called me early and said, "Get up and get me dressed and take me back to the hospital." We called in help to get him into the car and take him to the doctor. When we got to the office, my husband walked in. The doctor was so shocked to see him walking in his office that he ran out and got another doctor. They both looked at my husband's foot, and the broken one looked just like the other. The doctor said, "This is the one?" My husband said, "Yes." The doctor said, "Who did you talk to?" He said, "I talked to Jesus." The doctor said, "I don't know him but you stick with him. He did for your foot what we could not do."

They sent for the x-rays. They showed the foot's bones all mingled in with blood. They took new x-rays and put them next to the old ones, and the foot looked normal. God is the master of every situation. And I thank and praise God for his goodness, his kindness, and his mercy.

My Daughter's Pregnancy

My daughter also has a testimony of God's miraculous working power. During her first pregnancy, God spoke to me and said, "Don't give her a spinal." I knew nothing about spinals. But I told her to tell the doctor "no spinal." The doctor said alright. I told her God said to have the doctor write it down, and the doctor wrote it down. When she gave birth to her baby, during the labor, the interns were working on her, and they gave her a spinal. It paralyzed her from the top of her head to the bottom of her feet. She could not move her head or pat her own baby. They kept her at the hospital extra time, and it ran the doctor bill sky high. Because the baby was being breast fed, he had to stay with the mother the entire time.

Finally, the interns came out and told her husband what had happened. They had given her a spinal, and she would be in a wheelchair for the rest of her life. I asked her husband to let me bring her home with me. He said, "No. My father told me that a man was supposed to take care of his own wife." I said, "He taught you well. But, let me take her home to pray for her."

They brought her to my home. I pushed the twin beds together; I put her in one bed and the baby in the other. I anointed her and prayed for her three times a day: morning, noon, and night. Each time I prayed for her, I thanked God for her healing. She was still lying paralyzed; she couldn't even turn over. But the faith that I had in God caused me to thank him three times a day for her healing.

One day she called me to come upstairs. When I went up stairs, she could move her head and turn it inward. Another day she called me, and Glory to God, I went up the steps, and she could turn over in the bed. She called me another day; I ran up the stairs, and she was sitting up on the side of the bed. She said, "I feel that if you stand me on my feet, I could walk." I stood her up and she walked. She sat back down, got back up, and walked. She said, "Call my husband and tell him to come and take me home. God gave her complete victory." Five years later she gave birth to a healthy baby with no complications.

However, there was still that big bill left unpaid at the hospital. I fasted and prayed over that bill. I went to the hospital and talked to that manager at the desk. He said, "She'll have to pay the bill in full." I said, "Not so!" I went to the hospital manager. He asked me, "What do you think we should do?" I said, "Mark the bill paid in full." He said, "Whatever you say," and wrote on the bill "paid in full," because I could have sued them. But I was so thankful that God had given my child the victory. I'd rather see that victory than to have had a million dollars. God is the master of every situation. Both her children are grown. The boy is married, and the daughter is in her last year of college. I'm telling this for the glory of God.

My Son Raised From The Dead

The doctors had said that my late husband and I would never have children. Within a few months after adopting a girl, I found that I was with child, and this child was my son, Otis L. Boyd.

Deciding to follow his own pursuits, he did not choose to follow Christ. I had been requested to go to New Haven, Connecticut, for a meeting with Pastor Lulu Jackson. I had been gone for several weeks, having ministered in New York and Baltimore before going on to New Haven. I had just finished in New Haven, and because I was very tired, decided to remain a few days so that I might rest.

I had been fasting and praying for the young people and had just completed Monday, Tuesday, and Wednesday, when

God spoke to me and said "Pray for the children." Wednesday night, God spoke and said, "Fast Thursday and Friday for the children." Well, I had just fasted three days for the children, but I did not question God. I started fasting again. God did not have the saints in mind this time. He had my children, twelve-hundred miles from New Haven, at home in Indianapolis in mind, but I did not know that.

Early that Friday morning, before daybreak, the telephone began to ring in the home where I was staying. I knew when it rang, it was ringing for me. However, I was in a three-flat home in the middle flat, and I did not want to answer the telephone. But since nobody seemed to be answering it, I picked it up.

A newspaper article by the Indianapolis Recorder relating to the night club incident. Too bad they did not have all of the concluding information.

It was my girl in Indianapolis, and she said, "Otis has been cut very badly, and they are rushing him to the hospital. I will call you when we get there." I said to tell him that mother is praying for him and I'm on my way.

A drunk preacher had walked up to him between two and four Friday morning, when he and a group of friends were sitting around the table and said, "I'm going to put you in the morgue." He raised his knife and lifted one side of my son's nose off his face. The only thing that saved my son's eyes was that he threw his hand up. The preacher cut the two fingers and missed the eyes. While his hand was up on his face, the preacher stabbed him in the heart. He opened up the left side all the way down. When he fell over the table bleeding, the preacher stabbed him in the back, and the knife went all the way through the lung and cut the diaphragm in the front. They rushed my son to the hospital.

Back in New Haven, I got out of bed and began to pray. I stretched my life out before God and said to Him, "Lord, if I am in your will, I want you to do something. Lord, he is not worthy, but Lord, you are." God spoke to me and said, "I'll give him back to you." I did not understand what God meant when He said that.

I called the saints in New Haven, Connecticut and told them to come and get me. I got up and packed, drove to Jamaica, New York, picked up my ticket and flew to Indianapolis. They took me straight to the hospital.

Many people were at the hospital. They had taken time off their jobs after they heard on the radio that Otis Boyd, the hairdresser and model, had been cut to death. When I walked up, some of them fell into my arms and fainted. They asked me if I had talked to Otis' doctor. I said, "No I haven't talked to Otis's doctor, but I have talked to my doctor."

The doctors came in and took me to the room where they had washed and dressed him. They had sewed up his nose, taped up his fingers, covered him over, and waited for me to release him to the undertaker. When I walked in the room, the doctors and nurses were standing in a group; I guess they were waiting for me to pass out. When I walked up to him, I walked up from the back and just laid my hand on his shoulder and said, "Jesus!" When I called that name, his hand went up and he said, "Oh, mother don't leave me." I said, "Everything is going to be alright".

The doctors and nurses began to run. They said, "We're going to have to do something because the dead man is talking." They rushed him to surgery.

They cut him down the front and opened him up. God had sewed up the heart. God had sewed up the lungs. He left the diaphragm opened. I said to the doctor, "Do you know why God didn't sow it up? If he had sewed it up you would have thought that maybe the knife didn't go all the way through." He said, "Oh yes, the x-rays showed that the knife went all the way through."

The doctor said, "We want you to know that he is lucky." I said, "Not so doctor. He is blessed and we're not to take the credit from God." He said, "We're not going to say he's not going to die, but if he lives, he'll be an invalid in the wheelchair for the rest of his life." I said, "Not so doctor." My son looked at me and said, "Mother, I'm already an invalid. I can't move a toe or finger on my left side." The doctors said, "You never will move because every ligament and muscle is cut. When he opened up your side, he cut it." I called that same name,

Jesus, laid my hands on him again, and that left hand went up. It shocked the doctor, so he got up and stepped back from the table. He said, "I don't understand this case" and walked out.

They kept him there for almost a week trying to study his case. Finally, they said, "We don't understand the case; you can take him home." I had said to the saints that Saturday after he had been cut, "I will not eat or drink until he is sitting at this table with me." They said, "Don't say that." I said, "I've already said it." That Saturday morning, a week later, we sat down at the dining room table and ate together. Nobody had to cut his food. He cut and ate it all by himself. He's been well ever since.

The hospital actually gave me the death certificate, which had documented that Otis Boyd was dead. Today, he's saved, sanctified, married and has two wonderful daughters. This was the greatest miracle I saw God perform during my saved life. He is the master of every situation.

Section 2

The Testimony of Others

Mother Boyd with her sister, Viola Porter

Bishop Marion Shaw from Springfield, Mass at his church with Mother Boyd.

Arthritis

G reetings in the name of Jesus. I wanted to write to let you know how grateful I am for your prayers for my affliction. In June 1977, my doctor told me I might as well apply for disability because I had acute rheumatic arthritis, and I would never walk as before. I was then examined by two state orthopedic specialists. They agreed with my doctor's diagnosis. I was told to stay in bed, because if I fell, my bones were so brittle they would break.

In November 1977, I did fall, and my ankle bone and the fibula leading to the big toe broke. I asked Elder Lockett and the saints to pray for me. The Lord healed those bones in ten days, but I still could not walk. In March 1978, I decided not to take any more medicine or injections, but to keep on praying that I would walk.

On Friday, July 7, 1978, after your revival service, you said you would pray for 21 people who had been baptized in the name of Jesus and filled with the Holy Ghost. I could hardly make it to the line. I closed my eyes and prayed. You laid your hands on me and prayed for me to walk. The usher was helping me back to my seat when I realized I was walking. I did not need any help. I kept walking and praising the Lord. I did not want to sit down, and I have been walking ever since.

Yours in Christ,

Sister L. Moore
Springfield Gardens, Q.
August 1, 1978

Asthma

G reetings in the name of Jesus. I'm sure you will be surprised when you receive this letter, but nevertheless, I thank God for the opportunity to have you in our church and in our city from time to time. I always look forward to seeing you when you are in our city, as well as hearing you proclaim the Gospel of Our Lord and Savior Jesus Christ.

First of all, I would like to say that the first time I had the privilege of hearing you preach was when Pastor Lula Jackson, our Missionary State President, had you speak at one of our Missionary Conventions. Most of all, I thank God for when my pastor, Elder Redd, asked you to come to Ansonia, Connecticut, to our church to run a revival. It was about three years ago. This is when God touched my son, who at the time was about ten years old. He had chronic asthma, which had begun when he was about six years old. Just about every three months he would have these terrible attacks, and we would have to take him to the hospital. One night during the revival, you said you were going to give out prayer cloths (Acts 19:12).

Night after night, I sat and listened to the word of God coming forth and thought about the prayer cloths and wanted my son to be healed, and I brought him for prayer. I believe as the Scripture has said, that the prayers of the righteous availeth much. On the last night, I made my way to you and asked for a prayer cloth. After I told you about his condition, you gave me the cloth and told me to pin it to my son's pillow. When we got home, I did just as you said. This has been almost three years ago, and I thank God that I'm able to say he has not had another attack since.

Truly God is great and greatly to be praised. This is the second time since I've been saved that God has touched one of my children. Having a backslidden husband and six children to raise is not an easy task. But I thank God for Jesus and for his precious blood. For God has made me to know that He is God and that He ruleth in the kingdom of men.

Also, I would like for you to know that I thank God for you, for your ministry, and for the many sermons you preached to us on faith. I remember two in particular: "Lord Send Your Word" and "The Power of Prayer." I thank God that through your ministry, he healed my son's condition.

May God continue to bless you always. Pray for me and my family that God will save all of my children and give my husband a mind to be saved.

Yours in Christ,

Sister V. Ashe
New Haven, Connecticut

Cancer

L ate one afternoon I was leaving my home to go to my music theory class and felt the need to clear my throat. When I did so, I coughed up bloody mucous, then just clear blood. I thought it was probably a cold breaking up until a few days later, when I coughed up more blood. This had never happened to me before, so I thought I had better have a medical checkup, since I hadn't had one in a few years. The doctor ordered a chest X-ray that revealed a spot of some kind on my lung. The doctor seemed upset and started pacing the floor, afraid to tell me what the x-ray revealed. He finally told me of his findings and began a whole list of questions, such as: Do you smoke? Is there history of lung cancer or any kind of cancer in your family? He told me he had seen x-rays like that many times, and most of them were serious. There was one lady who refused surgery and was dead in a short time of lung cancer.

In the weeks that followed, I was in and out of labs for extensive testing. I also had one test, which had to be done in the operating room with three doctors in attendance. During my physical exam, he found a couple of other things that he felt might require surgery. He explained that the test he had ordered was a little complicated, and I needed a little anesthesia. This had to be done in the operating room.

After the test was completed, he came to my hospital room and told me the test was not successful in that it did not show anything. For a brief moment I began to thank and praise the Lord, thinking perhaps I was healed, when suddenly I felt like the Lord was saying "not yet." I felt a little sad but not troubled, because I prayed before I went into the hospital and had a few saints praying as well. I knew I was in God's hands and somehow He gave me the assurance that He was going to bring me out alright.

I was in the hospital three days. During that time, many doctors and specialists in their fields of medicine examined me. A lump had developed on my breast and also a nodule on my thyroid.

My doctor then expressed to me that since he was not able to determine just what the spot on the x-ray was, it was necessary for him to open me up and do a biopsy. He also said he could do three surgeries at one time. I continued to pray and ask the Lord to direct me in this very serious decision. I felt something compelling me to get up out of that bed and go home, but before I left, I had to be examined by the surgeon for the last time. He discovered the lump on my breast had begun to go down and that the nodule on my thyroid had begun to shrink. I began to praise God and thank Him because I knew He had heard and was answering my prayers.

During the weeks and months that followed, my doctor checked me and x-rayed me from time to time to see if the spot had changed. I was still refusing surgery. Every time he would ask me, I would say no. I told him I didn't make any decisions without asking God, and I felt he was leading me this way. He finally said to me one day, "I believe there is something to what you are saying, and I'm going to go with that." In the meantime, I talked to one of my prayer partners, who is a pulmonary lab technician, and she told me of a case similar to mine. After they performed a biopsy on a woman, they looked at it and still didn't know what it was. The woman became very weak and feeble and was still alive at that time, but I learned she died some time later. Thank God for prayer partners and God's people, who know how to pray and get in touch with God. She said to me, "Please don't let them do it to you." That just confirmed what I was already feeling, and I was satisfied the Lord had given me the answer for which I was looking. Not that I wouldn't have had the surgery, because I believe if the Lord had said surgery was necessary, I would have submitted to it. But I believe the Lord wanted me to have the testimony of His miraculous healing of my body.

I later went to a revival that Evangelist Boyd was holding at Ebenezer Chapel and talked to her after church. I told her of my problem. I didn't ask her to lay hands on me and pray then because it is not her practice to pray for anyone after dismissal. But I did solicit her prayers, and she advised me to trust the Lord and not let them open me up because whatever the outcome, they would say I'd just have to live with it. Not long after that, I went for another checkup, and the doctor looked at my X-ray and got all excited. He said, "Look, your X-ray is clear." He couldn't understand why I wasn't getting all excited like he was; but you see, I had gotten excited long before that when I started to turn it over to the Lord and completely trust in Him. I said, "The God I serve is certainly able to heal me, and if He isn't willing to heal me, I still know He is able, and I will forever trust in Him and believe Him and stand on His many promises."

He's the Master of Every Situation

The most beautiful thing about this experience wasn't the healing, but the wonderful way the Lord drew me closer to Him.

It seemed as though I was just shut away with Him and nothing else seemed to matter. Suddenly my healing wasn't so important to me as it had been before. I came to know the Lord as I had never known Him before and I loved Him more. Thank God I can now say of a surety that I know what God can and will do for us if we only put our trust in Him.

Sister C. Oliver
New Haven, CT

In 1963, I was very sick, sick to death, and I was in a terrible condition. People came to visit me and could not stay but five minutes in my room because the odor from my body was so bad. I had a friend who told me about Evangelist Mildred Boyd. My friend said, "I believe if you could get in touch with her and let her pray for you, I believe God would heal your body." I could not reach Evangelist Boyd the first time I called, but I continued to call her until I reached her and told her of my condition. Along with God and one prayer of faith, my body was healed. I never cease to praise God for His wonderful healing power.

Sister M. Blane

The Faith and Life of Mother Boyd

On July 31, 1978, the Lord saved me. I was scheduled to go into the hospital on August 16, 1978 for a pinched nerve and the removal of two discs. On Monday, the doctors ran several tests and x-rays, and they also told me that the operation would be on August 19 at 7:00 A.M. On Tuesday morning, they came in and told me I could go home because they could not find anything wrong. Elder Shaw prayed for me before I went in the hospital, and the Lord healed me through Elder Shaw.

In September 1982, I was ushering when the Lord revealed to Evangelist Boyd that I had a sickness all through my body. She asked permission from Elder Shaw to talk with me, and he gave her permission. She told me what God had showed her, and I told her that yes, I had cancer of my lungs and was going blind in my right eye. Evangelist Boyd prayed for me, and the Lord gave me my sight and stopped the spread of cancer in my lungs.

I went to the doctor in April of 1983, and he told me he had new drugs, which would cost $75.00 a dose. The Lord fixed it so my husband's insurance collapsed and I could not afford to take the treatments. Then the doctor took new x-rays to compare them with the old x-rays from 1982. The old x-rays showed where the cancer had spread to my heart and my good lung; but when the doctor looked at the new x-rays, he could not believe what he saw. He could not find anything.

I thank God for what He has done, because I know He is a healer. I would like for my testimony to be read because it might encourage someone else.

Sister D. Washington
Springfield, MA

He's the Master of Every Situation

O n March 4th, 1964, I had went to work at RCA when I became very ill. I thought I had indigestion, but later I became so weak I was sent home from work and advised to see my family physician. I went to see my family physician, realizing I was getting weaker. My family physician examined me and referred me to an internal medicine specialist. After examining me, the internist admitted me to the hospital and called in a gynecologist. After I had undergone several tests, the doctor told me that I had cancer. No words explain how I felt, because I had always dreaded the very thought of the disease. I called my husband and told him what the doctor had said, even how the cancer had eaten up the white blood cells. I was not given much hope; in fact, someone later told me that she wouldn't have given a dime for my life.

I had been blessed to live with a father and mother who were both sanctified and filled with the Holy Ghost, and I knew that there was a change in their lives. I also thanked God for a beautiful family of children, brothers, and sisters during this low period in my life. I thought I was not ready to be saved, but thank God for His lovingkindness and His tender mercy.

I remember one day Evangelist Mildred Boyd, after adhering to the voice of the Lord, came to visit me and prayed the prayer of faith. I was released from the hospital for two weeks on March 21, 1964, and that same night at 8:00, I went to Zion Tabernacle after talking with the late Elder C. Mills. I repented of my sins, was baptized in Jesus name for the remission of my sins, and God filled my soul with the Holy Ghost.

Thanks be to God. Bless His holy name. I thank God for this great woman of God, Evangelist Mildred Boyd, whom I did not know and had never seen before in my life. I am thankful to God that she came and prayed with me. I can say I thank God for saving me, for healing my body, and for keeping my husband and me saved and sanctified these twenty years and ten months - Bless His holy name.

I had many blood transfusions, but I'm so grateful I can say when the Lord saved my soul, I was connected with the blood giver, Jesus Christ.

I could go on and on, but there wouldn't be enough time to tell of all the goodness of God. Again I thank Him for healing my body and so many blessings I just cannot count them. The most beautiful thing I thank Him for is for saving my soul - that's why I'm saying constantly that I'm thankful. I thank God for putting blood back into my body, flesh on my bones - Bless His holy name.

I can say, "O give thanks unto the Lord for he is good and his mercy endureth forever."

Sister M. Brookins
Zion Tabernacle
Indianapolis, IN
October 15, 1966

Mother Boyd (left) at one of the first churches she preached at. She is wearing one of the many coats she made.

Deaf, Dumb, and Blind

The Lord has blessed me so many times through Evangelist Boyd that I would like to tell my testimonies. I had no sense of smell because of sinus and hay fever conditions. For years I couldn't smell anything. On October 10, 1968, I got in the prayer line, and Evangelist Boyd prayed for me. God healed me instantly; I've been able to smell ever since. It's an awful thing not to be able to smell, and I was always self-conscious of my body. I thank God for her and her prayer because I know that God uses, leads, and guides her.

In 1968 during our 1:00 prayer, I brought a little boy to church. He could not speak and was 4 years old. Evangelist Boyd prayed for him, and God opened his mouth. He began to talk and has been talking ever since. Through this, his sister was baptized and a demon was cast out of her.

Sister T. Stevenson
Ansonia, CT

P raise the Lord! I just wanted to send you my testimony of how the Lord is still in the healing business. Hallelujah! During one of our services held at Christ Church, I solicited your prayers concerning my eyesight. I had been to the doctor for my regular eye exam, and the doctor prescribed glasses for me. When I went to pick them up, praise God, they were too strong! The doctor asked me to wait until I got home and then wear them for two weeks, but I couldn't. Within seven days, I returned the glasses; the doctor again examined my eyes.

The doctor asked me to return the next week for another exam so that he might dilate my eyes for a more thorough exam. So I did. But my eyes stayed dilated for approximately two days. I also had a headache. I had received a prayer cloth from you when you had your annual revival at New Day Pentecostal Church. I applied it alternately on my eyes in the name of Jesus and my eyesight began to return to normal. I went back for a third eye exam, the next week. The doctor, praise God, was amazed! My eyes were totally healed. He said I have better than 20/20 vision. He also said that I could read the smallest line of letters entirely too fast, praise the Lord. I had been wearing glasses ever since the 4th grade. I am now thirty-two years old. "Only believe, all things are possible, if you only believe!" Praise God! I thank the Lord for your prayers. I thank Him for being a God of His Word. He's still in the healing business. I know because He healed me, and I thank Him. Continue to pray for me, Sister Boyd. Jesus is real! Hallelujah! I have better than 20/20 vision. I love Him. I get excited just writing about it!

The Faith and Life of Mother Boyd

God bless and keep on blessing you,

Love in Christ,

Sister V. Wilson
Jerusalem Temple
April 12, 1984

Mother Boyd at New Day Pentecost Church in Indianapolis, IN
where she did many revivals.

I n November 1981, the Lord healed my daughter's eye. Evangelist Boyd was preaching a weekend revival at our church ,and on the last night of the revival, Evangelist Boyd called for a baby with an eye problem. I did not respond to the call of the Lord. A friend of mine told me that she was calling for my daughter, but it was too late, for the altar call ended.

The next weekend, Evangelist Boyd was speaking in Lynn. I had called one of the sisters from the church there and told her about the night of the revival when the Lord called to heal my daughter, and I did not take her to the altar. She invited me to come to Bible class on Tuesday and to bring my daughter along with me. The Bible teaching started at 2:00, and I called my friends and told them to come also. I knew the Lord was giving me another chance to be blessed.

During the Bible teaching, a lady asked for prayer for her eyes, and Evangelist Boyd called her up. Everyone prayed the prayer of faith. Afterwards she called for my baby and said, "You have the baby with problems in the eye."

She said, "This is the baby I called for Sunday night?' I knew it was the Lord! Thank you Jesus. My baby had a spot in her pupil, and a hole was in it. She told me to believe that the Lord would heal my child. The church began to pray, and I prayed along with Evangelist Boyd, and the power of the Holy Ghost moved in the church. After praying, I looked in my child's eye, and the Lord had healed my baby. He had closed the pupil as if the hole had never been there. I had to thank the Lord for giving me another chance to bless my child.

Thank God for Evangelist Boyd being obedient to the Spirit of God. Pray that I will continue to praise the Lord and be obedient.

Sister S. Hall
Dorchester, MA

Diabetes

I would like to share with you what the Lord Jesus Christ has done for me and to help someone else to be obedient to His precious Word.

On September 26, 1963, I moved to Mississippi from Lewisburg, Tennessee. I went to work on the Indian Reservation on the 3rd of October. There I met and became friends with Sister M. Riddle and Sister Nettie Moore. I'd never been in contact with sanctified people before, but I knew there was something different about them.

Sister Moore encouraged me to attend church with her, and I was baptized in the precious name of Jesus and filled with the Holy Ghost. I have never felt anything like it before. It is a cleanness that I cannot accurately describe. On February 19, 1964, I met and heard Evangelist Mildred Boyd for the very first time.

Two weeks before I moved to Mississippi, Dr. Suellen Lee had diagnosed me with diabetes, high blood pressure, and being overweight (325 lbs.). I had also had surgery for cancer. I was taking two kinds of insulin twice daily, and my sugar checks were all running out of control. I listened to Evangelist Boyd teach and preach on faith and was amazed at all the wonderful miracles and miraculous things God had done for her and others through her. I truly believed, at that point, I was healed.

I stood up in the congregation of the righteous and received my healing. Evangelist Boyd prayed for me, and I went home to throw away my insulin.

That same night, because I was disobedient in another matter, I burned the fingers on my right hand with hot grease. Because I had been a nurse's aide for three years, I knew that I had third degree burns, but I never went to a doctor. I never stopped using my hand, but the fingers swelled up, popped open, ran, smelled, and hurt very badly. They hurt so badly that one day I went by Elder Jones' to get Evangelist Boyd to pray for them. While I was waiting for her to come out and pray for them, they simply stopped hurting. When Mother Boyd came out, I told her there was no need to pray because they had already stopped hurting.

The Evangelist was with us two weeks, and when she left, my fingers were healed. The color didn't come back, but it serves as a reminder to me of my disobedience to the Word of God. I threw away my insulin and needles because I truly believed I was healed. Sister Moore told me later that Mother Boyd had left word for me to go and have a check-up. Again I was disobedient, and I suffered many things. When she returned in 1965, I still had not done what I was told. Again she told me to go and get a check-up. On August 30, 1985 I went and had a check up. There was no sign of high blood pressure, I weighed 162 pounds, and my blood sugar was normal.

I suffered because I was disobedient. I had part of the victory because it had been three years since I had a drop of insulin. But because I was disobedient to what the Evangelist was telling me to do, I suffered all the rigors that the devil could bring upon me. Do whatever the Lord tells you to do, and do it with a sincere heart. God loves you, and He wants to bless you. I am now a very happy, healthy saint.

I praise God for Evangelist Boyd and her concern and caring for others, and I'll ever praise God for His Word.

C. M. Sanford

———————————————

I just want to thank God for Evangelist Boyd and how she teaches faith. For over 20 years, I suffered with diabetes and had to take insulin every day. In September 1972, Evangelist Boyd ran a revival in our church, and in noonday prayer, a thought came to me that I was tired of taking needles.

After I went home, I sat down, and the thought came again. The words dropped into my heart about what God could do. I said, "He can heal cancer, put bones together, and I believe He can heal my diabetes." So I spoke to Sister Boyd, and she said I was right, God could do all that and sugar was nothing to Him. As I testified about being healed, Evangelist Boyd was my witness, and she said God had healed me. I went back to the doctor in November. He tried to tell me that my sugar was worse and that my insulin should be increased. But I knew God had healed me. I thank God for faith to believe.

I'm still thanking God, for I haven't had a needle since September of 1972, and I feel so much better. I know Jesus healed me from diabetes and not only me, for when I testified of being healed my mother stretched out on faith and put down her needle in December 1972. It is no secret what God can do.

You pray for me in Jesus name, for I mean to go on in Christ Jesus.

Sister I. Lane

Epilepsy

The best thing that ever happened to me happened in the past 15 months. The first thing that happened was that I got saved in March. I was baptized in the name of the Lord and Savior Jesus Christ and received the gift of the Holy Ghost. Three months later, I met someone who stayed on my mind. Next to Jesus, she gave me so much spiritual encouragement.

She told me what to do if I wanted to be healthy. I had been a very sick man for 17 years with a disease called epilepsy. At times, I would have seizures three times a day. Sometimes I could not remember anything for three or four days. I had been to hospitals and medical centers all along the east coast. I had many brain wave tests, but the doctors couldn't determine what was causing this to happen to me. I took medication three times a day, but it didn't help. I feel so good now, that when I think of the condition I was in, I can't help but cry.

God sent Evangelist Boyd to me, thank you Jesus. She prayed for me, and God healed me instantly. No more pills, no more seizures. Thank God, I have been healed. I was healed through her prayer.

Brother E. Montgomery
Christ Church of Deliverance
Hartford, CT

Heart Attack and Strokes

P raise the Lord! I write to you to praise the Lord for His many blessings. On April 2, 1982, my husband, Louis Vaughn, suffered from cardiac arrest. He walked into the emergency room but never walked out. He also lost control of all bodily functions due to the lack of oxygen to his brain. He was in a coma and completely dependent on life sustaining machines.

Sometime in June, I stood in as a proxy for Louis as you, Evangelist Boyd, prayed a special healing prayer for him. Truly I can say that God is a good God, and that if one trusts and believes in the name of Jesus, nothing is impossible. When I returned to the hospital after your prayer, the nurse said that Louis finally showed signs of movement. His condition gradually improved. By July, the doctors had taken him off all the life support machines except for a humidifier and his intravenous feedings.

He was transferred to a nursing home on July 9, where he continued to get stronger. With physical and speech therapies, he soon began to talk, as well as feed himself again.

He's the Master of Every Situation

We decided to bring him home for the Christmas holidays. At that time Louis was still getting insulin shots. In the morning, I was to bring him home. The Lord performed another miracle, and the doctors told us that Louis no longer needed the insulin. Praise the Lord! Louis has been home ever since, and he's continuing to improve. He's talking more, sitting up in a chair, has gained his weight back, and they've recently closed his tracheotomy incision. God has truly blessed him and brought him a long way, even though the doctors had given up on Louis from the beginning.

I thank and praise the Lord for his many blessings and the power He has given you in His name.

Without the Lord and the prayers, Louis would not be where he is today. Please continue to pray for him and our family. Again, praise the Lord!

Sincerely Your Sister in Christ,

Sister Vaughn
September 4, 1983

Injury

F ollowing an automobile accident in August, 1981, I was diagnosed as having deterioration of the lower back muscles and assigned to wearing a back support brace with a prescription of pain pills and muscle relaxers. I soon tired of always wearing the brace and renewing the prescriptions. I made up my mind not to complain I simply told the Lord that as a relatively young man with a family, I would not like to live in this condition permanently if it was His will.

As the years progressed and the condition worsened, my spiritual desires increased and became more steadfast. I was determined to be the type of example that the Apostle Paul encouraged Timothy to be in 1 Timothy 4:12. Whatever I was to do concerning church work or outside the church, I did it without complaining. I believed that whatever I was doing, it was to be done unto the Lord (Colossians 3:17, 23).

Many times I would get home at night and rest awhile just to regain strength to get to bed. My wife would doctor me with heat, massages, and prayer. Many times she would ask me why I pushed so hard, knowing the pain that would follow. Yet deep down inside she knew it was because of my love and dedication to the Lord and sense of responsibility toward my family. Her love and concern prompted her to help me on many occasions.

He's the Master of Every Situation

I found inspiration through the word of God, our pastor's press in spite of his affliction, and the testimonies and songs of Zion. I awaken many mornings from what little sleep I am able to get and let the Lord know without His help, I would not be able to get up. He provides strength to my body and joy to my soul.

I learned to live a holy life in Christ Jesus or to be called a fool for Christ's sake. Rather I rejoice that I am one of the chosen ones. Whatever the Word of God says, I believe, even if I don't fully understand it. From the very first message you preached, I knew it would be a blessed week for me. I was so concerned in the spiritual aspect that the healing of my back did not cross my mind. I thank Jesus for His love towards me. Jesus spoke to me during the message on October and let me know that "tonight is your night for deliverance of your back." Sometimes you live with a condition so long that you think it as a passing thought. When you called the prayer gathering before the altar and told us to focus on one thing in our minds I focused on my back pain. When your hands touched my head, oh, Hallelujah! I don't know where the pain went, but I know it was not just a touch of relief but I thank God for counting me worthy to suffer to grant me another testimony of His reality. I thank you for doing business for the Lord and accepting the invitation to come and be with Gethsemane.

May our Savior and Lord Jesus Christ continue to richly bless and use you to His glory. Remember me in your prayers as I pray for you.

Deacon R. L. Howell
Indianapolis, IN
April 12, 1994

The Faith and Life of Mother Boyd

P raise the Lord and I thank God for you and His many marvelous works. Greetings to you this day, and may God bless you with continual good health and the peace of God.

I have joy today bubbling down in my soul. At last week's revival, it was out of obedience that I was at home. Therefore, when I heard that there was another week of revival, I felt that God had me in mind also.

The way was made clear for me to attend, I did what I could do at home by calling to invite the unsaved to the revival, and I prayed. When I saw that God had made the way clear for me to attend, I had purpose in my heart to be present every night. This included Monday night services; however, the revival began on Tuesday.

When the service was over, you called for me to come up in prayer. Truly, this request was a desire of my heart that I had made known to you, but I didn't expect to be called to the prayer line on Tuesday night. My mind was set on going up on Friday night for the prayer line.

When you laid hands on me, all my strength seemed to leave my body, and I collapsed. I could hear you saying, "God did it! God did it! God did it!" While I was still kneeling. I was so dizzy and felt so weak; but today, I know that surely "God did it." Today, I feel stronger and know that God has done a work in my body. I was able to pick up my 17-month-old son with no pain. No pain, Sister Boyd! God is truly a good, good God and I thank him for deliverance and for a woman of God who is used to save other people's lives.

Sister C. Robinson loves you.
January 13, 1983

I would like to say that we have a wonderful Lord and Savior. We hear people stand and testify how God has done wonderful things for them, and we know that it is the Lord. But we don't really know how wonderful He is until we are under attack, and the Lord brings us out as only He can. Then we don't just agree with what someone else is saying about the Lord, we know it then for ourselves.

Back in October 1985, I had really bad pains in my lower back. The pain was so bad that I was taking about six to eight pain pills a day just to get some rest. And even at that, I could only get two or three hours of sleep at a time. I sometimes laid on the floor, rubbed the backs of my legs, laid on an ironing board on the floor, and did other things to ease the pain. Finally, the pills stopped helping, so I went to see a doctor.

The doctor had some x-rays taken and said they showed that one of my discs had slipped. He said the disc had to be removed if I ever wanted to rest again without pain. I went to another doctor for a second opinion, and he said the disc in my back had shifted. Things had gotten worse, and my hopes of not having to go to surgery were slipping and shifting with the disc in my back.

The saints were calling and coming by, and everyone was praying with me and for me about my condition, but still the condition seemed to be getting worse. The Pastor, Elder Farris, came by and prayed for me; the Assistant Pastor, Elder Smith, came by and prayed for me; and then, Evangelist Boyd came by. She was there three days in a row, praying while she laid her hands right on the problem area where I hurt, and Wednesday I went to surgery. I say the Lord sent her. He sent everybody else who came, too, and still He sent her.

The doctors opened me up about 1:00 on Wednesday, and about 2:30 they told my family that except for some small arthritic problem in my back, there was no reason to operate. The Lord had already healed the slipped and shifted disc.

The doctors could not figure out what had happened. But thanks be to God for His healing virtue and the saints, who still believe that the effectual fervent prayers of the righteous avail much.

Praise God! I am healed.

Brother C. Hayes
Indianapolis, IN

He's the Master of Every Situation

There is power in the name of Jesus, and I am a living witness that prayer changes things. Twelve years ago, I was severely burned in a tragic automobile accident. My burns were so severe that it was necessary for the doctor to graft skin from the rest of my body to cover my burns.

The grafting seemed not to work, and finally, after the third attempt, the doctors said that there would be no more of my skin available, so they would have to use pigskin on my neck. That evening, Evangelist Boyd and Brother Jesse Humphries came to pray with me. As they prayed, I felt sure the Lord was going to answer their prayers. The next day, the doctors came in to check the skin graft, and to their surprise, it had grafted beautifully.

For six months I slept with my head over the foot of the bed, because by doing so, the skin would heal in such a way that my neck would be flexible and normal.

My experiences in this mishap were very rewarding. I learned to be patient and to wait on the Lord. He may not come when we want Him, but He is never late. Also, I am a living witness that there is power in the name of Jesus and that prayer does change things.

I thank and praise the Lord for all the miracles He has performed in my life. Please pray that my strength in the Lord is increased.

Brother C. Humphries

P raise the Lord. I am thanking God for a woman like you. It was your faith in God and your faith teaching that caused me to trust the Lord to heal me. God healed me of a throat condition I had in 1965 that could not be corrected by surgery. I thank God for the faith that I've obtained through your teachings. I could go on and on telling what the Lord has done for me, but the testimony I would like to share with others is about when God healed my son of a severe knee injury with torn ligaments.

In October 1973, my son Michael was injured while playing football for his high school team. The school had very good insurance for the boys and had some of the very best doctors. The school made an appointment with a bone specialist; I was told he was one of the best. I took my son to see the doctor, whose office was in Methodist Hospital. My son was in great pain and could hardly walk. When the doctor called him in to be examined, I remained in the waiting room.

After examining my son's leg, the doctor returned to the waiting room, wanting to talk to me. He said, "I've got some bad news. Your son must have surgery right away because the ligament in his knee is torn, and it takes surgery to correct it. He will be hospitalized for two weeks. Then he must wear a cast for five weeks." Many things ran through my mind. I thought after surgery there would still be the possibility of him walking with a limp forever. Or, it could even be worse than that. So I told the doctor that before I give my consent for him to do surgery, I would have to talk to someone else. When he saw that I really meant to talk to someone else, he said, "If you must talk to someone else, I suppose it could wait one more day. But when you bring him in the morning, make very sure that he doesn't eat anything, and he will go to surgery at 1:00.

As we left the hospital, I began to talk to my son. I reminded him of the many people God had healed right in our church. I also reminded him of a sermon Evangelist Boyd preached: "Can God Set Broken Bones?", and how God healed her husband's foot. I told him she said that her husband's foot was crushed, and that the bones and blood were mingled together. But God had set the bones and healed the foot without surgery.

I said, "God would do the same for you if you just believe." We went straight to Evangelist Boyd's house, and I told her what had happened to my son's leg and, that he was supposed to have surgery. I told her I didn't want him to have surgery, and I came so that she might pray for him. She looked at my son and told him he would really have to let his faith work. She began to pray, and God began to work. I could feel the power of God begin to work. I could feel the power of the Lord in that room. When she finished praying, she told my son, "I felt God working, son, and I know you did too! I want you to claim it by faith." She gave him two blessed cloths and told him to tape them on his knees.

When we got home, he did just as he was told, taping the blessed cloths on his knees. The next morning, I took him back to the hospital. I did what the doctors told me and hadn't allow my son to eat. He knew he was healed. The pain was gone, and he no longer had to limp when he walked. When the doctor called him to be admitted to the hospital, my son got up and walked toward the doctor. I've never in my life seen such an astonished look on anyone's face as the one on that doctor's face. He said, "Oh, you're walking as if there is no pain. I don't know how you can walk like that. It should be very painful." The doctor began to make excuses. He said maybe it really wasn't as bad as I thought, or maybe it was an old injury or an old sprain that re-occurred when my son fell. Then he said, "I cannot keep you because surgery is not needed. If it gives you any trouble, come back." My son looked at him and said, "I will not have to come back or have surgery."

We left the hospital thanking God for the miracle. I could hardly wait to get home so that I could call Evangelist Boyd and tell her the good news. When I told her all that had happened, we began praising God on the phone. She said, "I knew he was healed when I saw him last night at church, and I was hoping he had accepted it."

I thank God for healing my son through one prayer of faith from Evangelist Boyd.

Yours in Christ,

Bro. M. & B. Driver
Indianapolis, IN
December 15, 1973

He's the Master of Every Situation

Mother, when I called you, only God knew I was at the end. I felt like all my hope was gone. I had an operation on my leg and was in pain all the time. Sometimes I could not stand up or sit down. All I could do was stay in bed. The doctor said that whatever it was, it was spreading all over my body. My joints were coming apart. But after you prayed for me, I felt no pain.

I am thanking Jesus for your prayers.

May God ever bless you and bring you back here, and by the grace of God I will see you then.

Yours in Christ,

Sister V. Holmes
August 13, 1973

———————————

The Faith and Life of Mother Boyd

I am praising and thanking the Lord that he brought you to our church for revival. My back went out of place while you were here, you prayed for me, and the Lord put my back right in place. I came back home and did my housework.

Before, I had been to the doctor, who x-rayed my back and found that I had osteoporosis, which caused me to have complications. Vertebraes with foramina narrowing, posterior disc thinning, and short right leg with pelvic deficiency, which made me acquire liemboscaual joint (or wedging of the vertebra). So when my back would go out of place, the pain would be from my neck down to my foot on the right side. I could hardly walk.

I had been going to the doctor twice a week for three weeks, but it wouldn't stay in place. I had missed church for two weeks. My husband had to go to the store for me and help with the housework; plus I was in bad pain.

I'm thanking and praising God for healing my body completely. I went to church that night after you prayed for me. I got up to testify about my healing and ended up dancing up and down the church, when earlier I could hardly walk.

I'm thanking God for you Sister Boyd, for your love, concern, faith, and prayers, and I have found you to be a wonderful friend.

Sister J. Lucas
Brazil, IN
April 28, 1990

He's the Master of Every Situation

Praise the Lord. How are you? I'm feeling so much better since you prayed for me. For over a year, I've had trouble with my back. The pain was unbearable; my back felt as if it had no bone or support there. I couldn't stand very long and could only sleep on my back. I thought that I had what my father and uncles had a few years ago. The doctors said that I had Padgett's disease. It's a disease that caused all of my bones to deteriorate. My arms were so weak all the time, I couldn't hold them up, and my hands hurt to clap. I ached day in and day out. When I stood for long periods of time, I was in great pain, especially when I ushered. I would have to keep twisting or else sit down. I just thought it was something I had to live with.

I got in the prayer line for my back, but the Lord also touched my arms and hands. I thank God for since you prayed, I feel fine. I can clap now without pain. So far, I have walked without a limp. Please pray for me.

Love,

B. Rawls
New Haven, CT
1965

S hortly after I had my second child, I experienced difficulty bending over. I could only do so with great pain. In May 1984, a disc in my back slipped. Combined with my other back trouble, I was in tremendous pain. I was immobile for three days. By the fourth day, I was able to get out of bed and crawl. I thank God for my family during this time.

When I saw the doctor, he looked at me with great concern. My right leg had no reflex action at all, and my right foot had no feeling. He referred me to a neurosurgeon. Meanwhile, a friend mentioned a chiropractor who had helped his back. I made an appointment, thinking he could relieve some of my pain. He said I would need at least 24 treatments at $35.00 each. His office was 36 miles round trip from my home. Driving was very hard on my back. On one occasion, while driving home, I became disoriented due to the severe pain I was enduring.

I was seeing no improvement, so I decided to see another doctor. I made an appointment with a neurologist. He diagnosed my condition: I had a pinched nerve at the end of my spine. The only cure was surgery. However, he wanted to try cortisone shots first. I received two cortisone shots a week, which gave me little relief.

In July 1984, you arrived for a revival at Elder Tyson's church in Warren, Ohio. My condition was communicated to you, and you decided to come by my house and pray for me. I felt immediate relief. You left prayer cloths and explained how to use them. In a few days, I received complete deliverance! Oh, how I praise God that His healing power is still effective even in these faithless times. I also want to thank God for your ministry of faith, Evangelist Boyd. Your ministry is greatly needed these days.

May God bless you and your ministry,

P. Echols
Warren, Ohio
April 1985

Kidney and Gall Bladder Infections

L ast June, I became seriously ill, and the family decided to take me to the hospital; I didn't object. I felt my time was up. The next morning, I was ready to come home, but the doctors told my husband I had to be operated on. When they told me, I said no, that I didn't want to be operated on.

The doctors told my family that I had gallstones, that my gall bladder had burst, and that gangrene had set in. I was given only a fifty-fifty chance if they operated, and only a few days if they did not. So the family came and told me the operation was necessary. I was able to talk to Evangelist Boyd over the phone at the time; it's a good thing when you know someone who really has faith, regardless of the circumstances. My husband and family really wanted me to live, and they felt that if an operation would help, that was what was needed. After the operation, I was in intensive care for a few days.

Oh, I praise God for the faith of those who held on to God, and for all the prayers of God's people. He did hear and answer. Even though I was very sick for a while, the word went out, and saints were praying for me. Evangelist Boyd prayed and requested prayer for me everywhere she went. The prayers for

Mother Boyd was handing out one of her powerful prayer cloths during one of her revivals. God honored these prayer cloths even as he did the pieces taken from Paul's raiment, which were sent to heal people and deliver those possessed with devils (Acts 19:12). Many were healed by the use of the prayer clothes she gave.

the righteous availeth much. The doctors said that because I had been so sick, they were not able to get all the stones and would have to operate again in about three to six months.

After being home for a while, I began to feel better and asked the doctors to take the tube out of my side. They said they would not take the tube out until I had another operation. I began to tell others and called Evangelist Boyd and again asked for special prayer.

I wasn't going to be operated on again, but I wanted the Lord to either dissolve the stones or use whatever way He wanted to deliver me for His glory. I wanted God to heal me so that I would have a testimony. I also wanted the doctors to know that He heals without their help. God did just that. When I went in for x-rays, they were negative. God had done the work. And today, I am still rejoicing in the God of my salvation.

I can say with the Psalmist, "Bless the Lord, O my soul, and all that is within me, Bless His holy name. Bless the Lord, O my soul, and forget not all his benefits; who forgiveth all thine iniquities; who healeth all thy diseases; who redeemeth thy life from destruction" (Psalm 103:1-4).

My earnest desire is to continue to trust Him for His healing power, saving grace, and keeping power.

Sister N. Brooks
August 13, 1973

A bout four or five months ago, you sat in the hall by Elder Farris's office. I was leaving and stopped by and asked you to pray for a kidney condition. I had this condition for 16 years being dilated every three months.

Two months ago, I went to my doctor and was told there was no longer any infection in my bladder or kidney, and I didn't have to be dilated. I praise God because I was released from the doctor's care for the first time in 18 years. I thank you for your prayers.

Sister Paige
July 14, 1976

———————————

P raise the Lord and thank God for you and the miracle He performed through your praying. I just want to give you my testimony, how God healed me of a nervous stomach, which I had for 13 years. I could not eat anything and had to drink milk with strained egg white in it because it was the only thing that stayed on my stomach.

One night at your Revival, I had heard you read the testimony of Evangelist Rawls, and my condition was almost the same as hers. Therefore, I developed more faith that God has no limit to His miraculous power. When the prayer line was called, I entered it and that night, God healed me. I can eat anything I want to.

I thank God for you and for the wonderful miracle He has performed through your prayers.

Yours in Christ,

Sister M. Campbell

Pregnancy

I am writing this testimony to praise God for Mother Boyd, a true servant of God and a woman of great faith in God. Some eight years ago, the Lord laid it on Mother Boyd's heart to come to us in St. Charles, Missouri, where we had begun work for the Lord a year before. Then it was just Pastor, wife, three children, and two others. During these eight years, Mother Boyd has been faithfully coming to us holding a two-week Revival. The Lord has done great things in our midst, saving souls, and the teaching of faith in God, increasing our faith in God and His Word.

There are many miracles I can write about that the Lord has performed through this woman of God. There is one in particular that I'd like to share with you. It is one that I'll never forget.

This was in November 1967. I was 42 years old. We had children, three girls, ages 13, 16, and 22 years. I was expecting again, and my husband and I were quite happy. I had known my husband always wanted a boy, though he never said so. God had given us another chance. My prayer was Lord, let this one be a boy.

Then the enemy crept in, and I began hearing and reading things that happen to children and women my age. This fear was taking the joy of being able to bring forth another child.

Also, I was not well. I tired quickly, and was not able to eat. I didn't want anything. I was sick if I ate and sick if I did not eat. I was in bed most of the time.

When Mother Boyd came to us that November 1967, I was almost in the fourth month of my pregnancy.

We had not told her of my being pregnant, but she saw right away, and she too was happy. She said, "It's going to be a boy; I want to be the godmother."

The next morning, after the first night of the Revival, I was not able to get up to get my husband off to work. I did not tell him what was happening, but he knew something was wrong. He told me to stay in bed, that he could fix his breakfast and lunch. My oldest daughter came in the room because she had wondered why I was not up as usual. I told her I was in pain and bleeding. She immediately went and awakened Mother Boyd in the next room. Mother Boyd laid hands on me and said, "Believe God with me." She began to pray, and I began to believe God. The anointing of God was so powerful in my room I knew the work was complete. Glory to God. Mother Boyd sent my husband and oldest daughter off to work and the other two daughters off to school, and told them not to worry because I was alright. I stayed in bed the rest of the day, meditating and praising God for what He had done. That night I went to the Revival, rejoicing in my soul for the Lord had saved my baby. Hallelujah! I did not care then if the baby was a girl or a boy as long as it came here healthy and normal. Thanks be to God, I did not miss one night of the two-week Revival.

I wrote previously that I knew God's work was complete. I meant God not only saved my baby, but I was able to eat anything and go about my work around the house without tiring. Praise God! I can't begin to explain how good I felt to be able to eat and do things without having to make my way to the bed.

Also, to show you, myself, my hearers and readers, what a Mighty God we are serving, it makes me feel so unworthy of His Great Love, His deep concern, His tender mercies, and His faithfulness. That April, my oldest daughter got married. There was much to be done, even though it was a small wedding at home. We don't have a fine home, but what I have I like to keep nice. The Lord enabled me to wash windows, clean and wax floors, and cook a bridal dinner. This was my last month of pregnancy. The doctor said I had a few more weeks. The wedding was April 20, 1968, and our boy (praise God) came here April 22, 1968. A healthy, normal, 6 ½ lb. boy. God gave us the desires of our hearts. We wanted a boy, then later just a healthy normal child. But God, hallelujah, gave us all three a boy, healthy, and normal.

This is just one of many reasons I thank God for Mother Boyd. I thank God for every remembrance of her, always in every prayer.

I am thankful for the good work He began in her; may it continue until His appearing.

Sister F. Watts
St. Charles, MO
June 1975

The Faith and Life of Mother Boyd

This letter is being written to you by my husband and myself to say "thank you" once again for your many words of encouragement and prayers for us during my rather difficult pregnancy. We also hope that you will be able to use our testimony in various travels to help someone else who might have the same problems that we had. I have told other saints about it, and they also encouraged me to write this testimony.

My husband and I had already lost one child, and I desperately wanted another. Our Pastor, Elder Farris, had called the church on Solemn Assembly and told the congregation to put their prayer requests all in a large box together, and the Lord would answer each one of them if we had enough faith to believe. Two months later, the Lord answered our request when we found out that we would be blessed with another child in June. However, after running a few tests, the doctor told us that I only had a 5% chance of carrying the child. He went on to say that he thought this child had died because no heartbeat could be found, and there was no sign of life. He advised me to have an abortion, because I would be endangering my life if I tried to carry the child any longer. I refused to go along with this because Elder Farris told me to remember "God can do great things."

A month later, my husband and I attended your Revival at New Day Pentecostal Church. You asked for two prayer lines consisting of ten people in each line. I was sitting in the choir box and could not get in line. However, you went on to tell how if we had enough faith, we could be healed as we sat in our seats. As you began to pray, I put my hands on my stomach, and my baby began to move and continued to do so for the next six months. That was the same night that you suffered two heart attacks and a stroke, and the Lord also touched your body.

As time went on, the doctor began to worry because I had not given birth and the baby was long overdue. He began to talk about taking the baby by Caesarean section. I talked to you about this, and you prayed for me and gave me a prayer cloth. I wore the prayer cloth for a while and then gave it to an unsaved friend of mine whom the doctors thought had cancer. I told her that God could heal her too. She went into the hospital, and no cancer could be found. Two months later, the Lord blessed us with a beautiful healthy son. The doctor ran tests on him because she was afraid that I had carried him too long, and that he might have birth defects because of it. All the tests came back negative, and she had to admit that he was just fine. His doctor now says he is one of the healthiest and largest babies that she takes care of.

Evangelist Boyd, we will never be able to repay you. It is because of your prayers and God's great mercy and love for us that my husband and I now have the child we have always wanted.

Yours In Christ,

Brother and Sister W. Smith
February 1, 1981

P raise the Lord! I greet you in the precious name of Jesus. Many times I have heard you say, "Can God? God Can!" I can truly say today without a shadow of a doubt, God can do anything - but fail! In December 1964, I went to the doctor for a physical examination because I was feeling extremely tired and weak. Much to my surprise, the doctor told me I was expecting a child. Needless to say, I was not very happy about this because I had been married 11 years and was approaching 27 years of age. I felt like I was too old to have a child. I called Evangelist Boyd to share the news with her because she has known me most of my life, and she and my mother were very good friends.

When I told her, she gave a little shout over the phone, "Baby...I am so happy for you. Isn't God good? I prayed when you got married 11 years ago that God would give you and your husband a child. Aren't you happy?" When I didn't respond to her question, she picked up on my depressed spirit. Very little gets by Evangelist Boyd. I began to tell her I felt like I was too old to have a child. She quietly began to talk with me and let me know that God never makes a mistake. "Lift your head up and praise the Lord. There are many people who cannot have children. Many people are trying to adopt and buy through the black market. You should be grateful. Repent right now and ask God to forgive you." I thank God for Sister Boyd's honesty she really let me see myself.

As my pregnancy progressed, complications developed. The doctor discovered fibroid tumors eight years ago and told me that I would eventually have to have a major operation to remove them. However, these tumors had been continually growing, and one was growing with the baby and causing great pain. The pain was excruciating.

At the beginning of my fifth month, the doctor made arrangements for me to go to the hospital for tests. Because of my age, he suggested I take a test called amniocentesis. It would determine if the baby was abnormal, the position of the child, the position of the tumor, and the sex of the child. The test results showed that the child was normal. However, it was in breech position, and the tumor was very large and was growing against the baby.

The doctor informed me that because of the size of the tumor and the position of the baby, I would not be able to carry the baby full term. I would have to have a Caesarean section.

As I progressed into my sixth month, the pain grew worse, so much at times I had to grab hold of the headboard of my bed and just scream. I was extremely worried and prayed continually. However, the pain continued. I had only gained two pounds, and my strength was almost gone because I could not keep anything down. The doctor suggested taking the child. I told him no, God is going to work a miracle. He looked at me strangely.

One evening my husband came to my bedside very worried, and I began to encourage him. I told him I would call Evangelist Boyd. I knew she had been out of town for a while, but my sister had called me and told me she was back home. I called Sister Boyd and she said she would come over. Before she anointed and laid hands on me, she ministered to me with Scripture and quietly began to talk with me. I believed God. I did not feel immediate relief, but I knew that God had done the work.

As I approached my eighth month, the baby was still in breech position, and the doctor would not turn the baby because of the vastness of the tumor. I still believed God was going to perform a miracle. God said it, I believe it, and that settles it. Two weeks before I was actually to deliver, God started labor. I went to the hospital, and the doctors were set up to do a Caesarian section.

One of the specialists who had been called in on the case told my doctor that before going ahead and doing a c-section, they should take x-rays to be sure the baby was still in breech position (it was still in breech the week before). They took the x-rays, got the results back in 20 minutes, and God had done the work. The baby had turned into normal position to be delivered into the birth canal, and the tumor had shrunk. The Lord let the baby come so fast.

From the time I left home on July 19, 1985, I had the child within four hours, with no pain killer, and I was wheeled back into the recovery room within one hour and talking to as many Saints as I could to tell what my God has done. I thank God for a faith-teaching and believing woman like Evangelist Boyd.

Evangelist Boyd, may God continue to bless and keep you and your days be long.

"Can God? God can do anything - but fail"

"Thank God for my beautiful Baby boy."

Sister D. Golder
Indianapolis, IN
November 12, 1985

Sickle Cell Anemia

In 1971, my son, Bruce Shaw, became very sick. He would wake up in the morning with pains in his stomach so bad, that some days he was not able to go to school. This went on for a long time, and then he got a sore on his leg that looked as if it would never heal.

I decided to take him to the doctor. After the doctor had examined him, he told me my son should have a blood test taken, which he did. As it turned out, my son had sickle cell anemia. His blood count was very low, and food just did not appeal to him.

The doctor told me he was never to fly. But thank God for such a woman of God, Evangelist Boyd. When I told her about the condition, she said there was nothing impossible with God. She prayed for Bruce and gave me some healing cloths for him. He was healed of the condition. Thank you, Jesus.

When I took Bruce back for a check-up, the doctor was surprised because Bruce's blood count was normal. The sore healed, and Bruce has been eating ever since. When the convention was in Milwaukee, my husband took Bruce on the plane, and he did not have any trouble at all. I thank God for Evangelist Boyd. She has helped my family in so many ways, and as I have so often heard her say, sometimes the condition seems like it gets worse before better, but God can do anything but fail.

Sister B. Shaw

When the Doctors Did Not Know

At the age of nine, I became very ill with a fever, which the doctor said was rheumatic fever. For the first year of the illness, I received penicillin shots often. As time went on, I was still very sick, but could not find out what was wrong. Eleven years later, I became ill again. No one could say what my problems were. I went to various hospitals and clinics, but to no avail. My problems continued until I was rushed to Methodist Hospital because I had suffered a heart attack. The doctor explained that he wanted me to walk a mile in the morning and a mile at night after I was released from the hospital. At this time, I had a reoccurrence of the old illness. The heart specialist requested I see another doctor.

From the first of 1988 until July 31, 1988, I became very ill. I was unable to tie my shoes, button my clothes, or roll my hair because I couldn't raise my hands above my head. Walking and standing became problems. I was off work a lot before 1988, but July 1988 was my last month working. I went to see the doctor, and he gave me a letter to send to work because I was unable to work at that time.

On January 1, 1989, I went to Victory Tabernacle and was baptized in Jesus's name and received the gift of the Holy Ghost. That same month, the doctor gave me another letter saying I was still unable to return to work. But on Friday, May 26, 1989, during a Revival at my church, Evangelist Boyd prayed for me after delivering a message on faith. Having the faith for my healing, He healed my body, and now I'm doing things I haven't done in years. I praise God because he kept me and healed my body, and I intend to walk with Him all the way. All we have to do is trust God, believe, and receive.

God bless Sister Boyd.

Your Sister in Christ,

W. Harrison
Indianapolis, IN

More Miracles

I met Evangelist Boyd many years ago and found her to be a true child of God, very dedicated in the work of the Lord Jesus. We worshipped the Lord together at Zion Tabernacle, which is our home church. Elder Plummer and I began Saturday night prayer meetings in our home, which many saints attended.

Elder Plummer and I had to go to Georgia to get my mother, who was sick and under the doctor's care and crippled by arthritis. We brought my mother back, and the doctor told her she would live only about five years, even if she took the medicine prescribed for her. I told my mother her life was in God's hands, and she must try Jesus as her doctor. She was filled with the Holy Ghost, but had not been baptized in Jesus's name.

On Saturday night, when the prayer band came to our home, my mother would stay upstairs and listen to the service because she couldn't walk down the basement steps. She would have to slide down like a baby, because she was afraid that even with the aid of a stick in one hand and someone else holding the other hand, she would fall.

One Saturday night the power of the Lord was so great, and Evangelist Boyd asked, "Where is your mother?" I told her she was listening upstairs, and she said, "Send and get her and come down, she'll be able to walk." Dolores, who is my oldest daughter, brought my mother down part of the way, and Evangelist Boyd met her and reached for her hand; mother came the rest of the way. Evangelist Boyd told everyone to pray, and told mother to walk up and down the basement steps and believe God. Mother went up and down several times without any help. She put the stick down! She was baptized in Jesus's name and put the doctor and the pills down. Jesus has been her doctor ever since, and that was in 1962, ten years ago. She is eighty years old now, and is very active and baby sits for my daughter and sometimes for other people. Praise the Lord for his mighty power.

During this same prayer band, my youngest son, Kevin, was a baby at the time, about two years old. He was stricken with a cold that left him with a condition where he could not breathe out of his nose. We sat up night after night and nothing seemed to do any good.

One Saturday night down in prayer, I was holding the baby in my arms while kneeling at a chair. I felt someone touch me; it was Evangelist Boyd. She told me the Lord said if she would blow in his mouth, He would heal Him, and she wanted to know if it was alright. I told her yes. She took Kevin in her arms, and he was burning up with fever. She blew in his mouth, and he began to breathe normally. The mighty power of God healed him! His fever broke, his color came back, and his breathing was normal. He has been running around ever since. I told Evangelist Boyd sometimes I feel she needs to pray for him to slow down. Thank you Jesus!

I also had a son, Ralph, go to Korea. He was over there about 18 months and was due to come home for Christmas. It was at this time that Russia moved missiles into Cuba and all military leaves were cancelled. We had a prayer box where we put our requests, and no one opened them to read them. We would just pray over them. I wanted my son to come home. What I am about to say may sound foolish to some, but I sat down and wrote a letter to Jesus. It began with "Dear Jesus," and I told him all about our trouble. I put it in an envelope and addressed it to Jesus in Heaven. Jesus also told me to write my son a letter and tell him that God was still on the throne. I told Evangelist Boyd what had happened, and she said, "Believe God." I told the saints my son was coming home. Some looked at me with pity; some probably thought I was losing my mind, because I was broadcasting it everywhere. It had been declared that no one could go home. On December 23rd, about five o'clock in the morning, my phone rang. I answered it, and it was my son. He was in Indianapolis and asked us to pick him up. I jumped up and stood up in bed, praising God for this miracle. My son told us his commanding officer came to him and said, "Plummer, I have booked passage for you to America, the only stop will be Japan." He also said he was the only soldier to leave. The others were amazed, but we know it was the mighty power of God.

Concerning myself, I had a thyroid condition. My neck was protruding, my eyes bulging out of my head, rheumatoid arthritis, pneumonia, and influenza, all of these conditions. I also had rheumatic fever, which caused me to have a bad heart condition. At night I would have to sleep on two or three pillows, and sometimes I was unable to sleep or breathe. My husband would have to open the doors and windows in zero degree weather for me and pray for me and with me.

I had purposed in my heart to trust God. I was called crazy.

The Faith and Life of Mother Boyd

The doctor wanted to operate on my thyroid, and I told him no. The Lord let me go downtown one day, and I met a lady I had never seen before. She came over to me, and she said, "You have a thyroid condition, don't you?" I said yes. She said she had one, and had surgery for it, and now it is growing back. I told her I wasn't going to have an operation. Evangelist Boyd told me to anoint my throat every day with the blessed oil and believe God, and surely He did everything He said He would. He operated on my throat and didn't even leave a scar. He put my eyes back in my head and did what no doctor could every do. Bless his holy name!

I would call Evangelist Boyd in the morning, sometimes at noon, night, and even midnight or two, three, or four o'clock in the morning. But whatever time I called, she was never too sleepy, never too busy to pray for me. She even came to my house more often than you would ever be able to get a doctor. Who wouldn't appreciate her? My legs were so swollen they were out of shape and looked inhuman. They looked like some type of animal leg, like elephant legs.

When Evangelist Boyd came to pray for me, I couldn't even walk. I couldn't even stand a finger touch at first. But as she begged the Lord to undertake, you could see the swelling going down, and as she moved her hand on my legs, the swelling would move down a little further, until finally it went to my feet and didn't want to move. But she said the devil is a liar, and we believed the Lord would do the work; and He did.

Today, we are grateful to God for the faith Mother Boyd has taught us and still teaches us. Truly our desire is to be steadfast and immovable in God. Some move with everything that comes along, but we praise the Lord for the faith that Evangelist Boyd teaches, for every soul that she has helped to be saved. Truly, I can safely say, "God is our refuge and strength, a very present help in trouble." Elder Plummer and I, also my family, are living witnesses of what faith can do. It can move mountains! Our church was named Faith, because we were by faith and not by sight. Elder Plummer, the saints of Faith, and I do appreciate everything Evangelist Boyd has done, and we are praying God will bless her to do greater works, although I wonder what greater works she can do.

Sister Plummer
Columbus, Ohio
November 21, 1978

Section 3

Deliverance & More

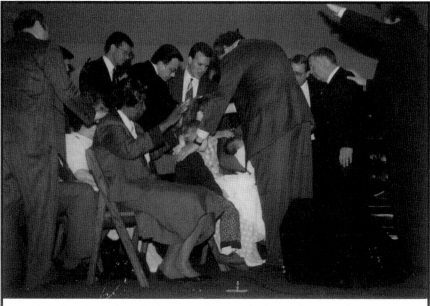

Mother Boyd at Calvary Tabernacle in Indianapolis, IN.

Finances

My husband and I were up against a loan company. If we did not pay the debt, they were going to sell our home. For all the saints who are worrying about Reaganomics, I'm a living witness that there is no shortage in God. The loan company was demanding the sum of $2,635.44. For those who have bank accounts with a savings, that would not be a problem, but we had nothing in an account. We had only a few weeks to get this money together, and by having just moved to a new city, we had no one to turn to. But look what Jesus can do. He blessed me to get a job as a private duty nurse for a very rich family in our city.

The lady of the household fell in love with me. So one day, one of the sons said he wanted to give me a gift. So I said, "I can't accept cash from any clients, I must be honest." He said, "I must be legal, the United States law says I can give you a gift anywhere from $1.00 - $3,000.00 tax-free money." Look at Jesus! We were able to pay the debt of $2,635.44. Praise God, but that is not all.

One of the sons is a prominent lawyer in the city and has the Holy Ghost, and he met me. I am now his private duty nurse. Each week after taxes, I bring home at least $1,000.00 clear money. To God be the glory!

He's the Master of Every Situation

I praise God for Evangelist Boyd, for her prayers put me in nursing school. One Christmas Day before I was married, she had about five or six of the young adult single sisters over to her house, and she taught us Bible study and prayed for us. I believe I was the only one who did not ask for a husband. I wanted to be a nurse. The Lord blessed me through that prayer. I say that prayer because I applied one and a half days before school started with 11 people on the waiting list and NO MONEY! I started school one day late and still no money. The receptionist said something happened to each one of those people ahead of me. Even one person's house caught on fire. So that's why it was Evangelist Boyd's prayer that put me in school and kept me there. The Lord blessed me with a truly saved companion who loves the Lord, so you know he loves me.

So often we say, "One person cannot pray any better than I can, or God can use me like He uses her." You know the entire saying we have in holiness. Is that why Evangelist Boyd's phone rings constantly, 3:00 and 4:00 A.M. I know this lady has a special place in God's heart, her prayers and works alone show that. I praise God for giving her to us.

"But a woman who feareth the Lord, she shall be praised. Give her all of the fruit of her hands, and let her own works praise her in the gates" (Proverbs 31:30 - 21).

Humbly submitted,

Sister C. Wright

The Faith and Life of Mother Boyd

P raises to the wonderful name of Jesus, to whom I owe this testimony. A month ago, you were running a Revival in Chicago. I came through the prayer line. You prayed the Lord would bless me with a miracle. From that night I started believing and thanking God for it.

I began to ask the Lord for a car to get to church. I went to look for this car with 37 cents in my purse. I found a 1973 Vega, just what I wanted. I told the man I'd be back with the full amount from the car. When I got home, a man called me and told me to pick up a check for $1,337.93. I also must add he called me three times to make sure I was coming to get the money. Also, I had my car insured three days before I even picked the car up, and I hadn't paid the first premium until three days after I got the car.

I thank God for Sister Boyd. I thank God for the money. I thank God for the car. But most of all I thank God for Jesus.

Sister Boyd, I love you, and I pray that some day I have the great faith you have in God.

Sister L. Campbell
Chicago, Illinois

Relationships

I would like to take this opportunity to share with you my testimony of what God has done in my life for His glory and His namesake, and I pray that when you hear it, your faith will be increased in the great God of our salvation.

I came to know about the Lord at the age of 16 years old. I had been baptized in Jesus's name, but I was not filled with the Holy Ghost. For four years, I tarried and tarried and could not receive the Holy Ghost. I did not realize that it is a gift, and I did not have to work for it. Eventually, I gave up because adversity that I could not handle had come upon me.

Within six years, my life was completely messed up. I had gotten involved with a man, and we started living together. We had two children, and we were happy because we loved each other, but deep down in my heart I wanted to be saved. He also expressed the same feelings. We wanted to get married, but we could not because of circumstances, but we both knew that the way we were living would not please God.

You see, what we were trying to do was fix things for ourselves before we came to God, but praise God for the word of grace that said come as you are. I thank Him that He never gave up on me. I felt I could not leave this man because we had established ourselves together, and we loved each other; plus, we had our children. We did not have a quarrel to make me pack up and leave, and I had no money or a place to go, but the Lord kept saying, "Seek ye first the kingdom of God and His righteousness and all these things shall be added unto you."

Then God made me realize that I was putting this man before Him, and I made up my mind then that no matter what it took, I was going to serve the Lord. I packed up my children and moved in with a sister in our church after God had wondrously saved me, and somehow, that man turned into the meanest thing you could imagine. He did everything He could to make me come back to him, but I was determined to walk with the Lord.

Not very long afterwards, Sister Boyd, you came to our city for our annual Revival, and when I met you and heard you preach, I knew that you were a woman of God; and the saints had told me so much about you.

I came to you one day just perplexed and crying, and I told you how I could not find a job to take care of myself and my children who, when not in school, stayed at the house when I needed to work. The sister whose house I was staying at had to move, and the bank that owned the house ordered me to leave. I said to you, "Mother Boyd, all of this makes me feel like the children of Israel with mountains on either side, the Red Sea before me, and the man like Pharaoh behind me." You said, "Whatever you do, don't give up, because God is able, and He will not hold any good thing from them that walk uprightly before Him." You prayed for me and told me that God would work a miracle for me if I held on and trusted Him. I gave you a letter I had received from a place I had applied for a job, and asked you to keep and pray over it for me. You brought the letter back and told me to expect God to work.

He's the Master of Every Situation

The same day that my baby was to be dismissed from the nursery, God gave me a job. I don't know if you realize what it meant to me for my baby to stay at nursery school. If he had been dismissed, I would not have had a place to leave him, but God gave me victory there. Soon afterwards, God gave me an apartment. It was in the cold of November, and I had no heat in my other place, but this apartment had heat turned on before I even went there. Praise God! Not only that, but two years later, the man I had given up to walk with the Lord was baptized in Jesus's name, and God filled him with the Holy Ghost.

He told me after he was saved that he watched to see if I was going to turn back, but my determination made him decide that he wanted to be saved. After I watched him walk with the Lord in spirit and in truth, I said yes to his proposal of marriage. June 13, 1982 was our first anniversary, and on the 22nd of the same month, we had our brand new baby boy, our third son. Today, three months later, I am a homemaker and a full-time wife and mother, and I am very, very happy in the Lord Jesus.

I thank God for having met you. You are a great woman of God who taught me faith in God and to watch him work things out in my life. Praise God.

B. Foreman
Springfield, MA
October 1, 1982

Spiritual Deliverance and Cancer...

My illness started as a sore throat in January 1970. I was so sick I decided I would see a doctor. He told me it was only a sore throat and gave me a bottle of Cepacol mouthwash to gargle. This I did, but it got worse. I went to the eye, ear, nose and throat hospital, where about seven or eight doctors looked at me. Finally, one came and said that it looked like cancer. They were not sure and wanted to perform a biopsy. I agreed, and the biopsy showed that I did have cancer. They wanted to operate in September 1970, but I told them to let me think about it. After fasting and praying, I decided not to let them operate. Everybody was glad that I said no, because the air would only make it spread all over my body. So you can see that operating was the furthest thing from my mind.

In January 1971, I was no better I kept getting worse. A friend told me about Katherine Kuhlman, who was having a meeting in Philadelphia that February. I went to the meeting, praying all the way there. I saw many miracles, but nothing happened to me. I came back just the way I had left. I kept praying, but it seemed the more I prayed, the worse I got. Finally I gave up. I came to the end and said, "Lord, thy will be done, I know I am going to die." Satan said, "Yes, you sure are going to die."

He's the Master of Every Situation

One day I was sitting thinking about my condition when the phone rang. It was Sister Ethel Maddox, who said the Lord had laid it on her heart to call me. It had to be the Lord Jesus because I had not talked to her in about a year and a half. After I told her of my condition, she asked if she and Sister Ollie Lafayette could come and visit me. I told her they certainly could. Thank You, Jesus. They came and showed me in God's Word that I was not saved. This upset me because I had been baptized in the name of the Father, Son, and Holy Ghost and went to church every Sunday. I was president of the Usher Board. As a matter of fact, we had all belonged to the same church at one time. Thank you, Jesus. They said that they were not saved then either. Naturally, it didn't sound good to me, but Jesus knew that I wanted to be saved. They showed me Acts 2:38 and invited me to the Morgan Park Assembly Church.

This was in March 1971. I was baptized in Jesus's name, just like the Word said. I thank the Lord for letting me obey His Word. I read that obedience is better than sacrifice. Satan really got busy, and my throat really got worse; I started spitting up blood. I still wanted to be saved, but I didn't know what repent meant. I thought getting baptized was all. I was tarrying for the Holy Ghost. I said "Lord, I am your child, please fill me with the Holy Ghost." He let me know that I was not really His child, I was nothing but a sinner. That's when I repented and asked Him to forgive me of all my sins.

Satan really doesn't want to see people saved and will do all he can to hinder them. My voice became a very low whisper. I could hardly breathe. My breathing passages had closed up, all but one. My husband rushed me to the hospital one Monday night, and they operated the next morning in order to force my breathing. The next few days I had to take about five radium treatments. They operated and removed the voice box. I couldn't make a sound or utter a word.

One thing I knew, I wanted the Lord to save my soul. I asked Him, "Please save me." I wasn't concerned about my voice. I was thinking about what good is my voice, if I die and lose my soul. Thank you, Jesus. He filled me with the Holy Ghost and gave me a new voice. No man could have done that, only Jesus.

What a mighty God we serve. I have seen people with cancer who suffered and became skin and bones. I feel just fine. Thank you, Lord, no pains and no medicine. The miracle didn't happen at Katherine Kuhlman's meeting, the way I thought it would, but God's way is always the best way.

The greatest miracle of all happened when the Lord saved my soul and filled me with the Holy Ghost in June 1971. I thought I was living, but I was only existing.

You have never lived until you obey God's Word and let Him fill you with the Holy Ghost. Going to church every Sunday and holding a position like I was is not going to save us. We must obey God's Word and repent and be baptized in the name of Jesus for the remission of sin, and we shall receive the gift of the Holy Ghost.

The name of Jesus Christ, not Father, Son, and Holy Ghost. Those are titles, not names, and there is no salvation in any other name but Jesus. There is no other name under heaven given among men whereby we can be saved (Acts 4:12). Thank you, Jesus. As I sit and look back over my life, I can truly say the Lord has brought me a very long way. This is just a light summary of some of the things the Lord has done for me. It's impossible to tell it all. I can truly say, "Living for Jesus gets sweeter and sweeter as the days go by." When the Lord fills you with the Holy Ghost, it makes you love everybody and be concerned about others. My prayer is that the Lord saves sinners and heals the afflicted, and that I will be meek and humble and be the saint He wants me to be.

Sister W. L. Dixon
October 31, 1986

Spiritual Deliverance and High Blood Pressure...

I would like to praise the Lord, for He healed me of high blood pressure in 1966. There was a Revival going on in the city of New Haven, Connecticut. I was told there was a woman evangelist, and that she was a great speaker. So I decided to go and see what was going on. When I went to the service that night, I did not know I needed salvation and had never been told that the Lord could heal my condition. As I sat in the service and heard the saints praising God for what He had done for them, I began to believe the Lord would do the same for me. At that time, I was seeing a doctor two to three times a week and was taking ten different pills everyday. I was very tired of swallowing pills, but the doctor said I must not miss taking any of them, so I did what he said. As Evangelist Mildred Boyd brought the Word forth that night and she made the altar call, I really did not understand her messages, but I just believed what she said. I took on the name of Jesus by water baptism, and I believed the work was done that night because I obeyed. The Lord blessed my soul really well. I just went home and threw away every pill in the house. The Lord filled me with the Holy Ghost ten days later, and I knew He was a healer. I never took another pill for my blood pressure, and when I started in Jesus's name, my blood pressure was 222.

You know I witnessed, God is a wonder in my life, I was healed, and today I can still claim victory in His name.

Sister A. Vaughn
New Haven, CT

Section 4

In Loving Memory of Mother

Mother Boyd with her son, Otis Boyd.

A Tribute To My Mother

Growing up in a strict Christian environment seems like such a boring life to many, but in my household, there was always peace in the valley for me. In the early years of my childhood, it seemed we always had company on Sunday for dinner or someone coming by for counseling. My mother would go out of her way to help someone in any way that she could, but you had to listen to her once she gave you the advice.

My mother could sit down with you and explain the Bible to you at whatever level you were with God. She never tired of talking about God and his promises to his people. If you needed encouragement, she was the person to talk to. I don't remember a time in my life when Evangelist Boyd would not put her own cares aside for someone else's. If she promised to do something for you, you could consider it done. She truly was a person of her word.

Nothing kept her from her responsibilities as a wife and mother. Whatever she had to do, you could be assured that she had taken care of or made arrangements for her family to be taken care of first. She very rarely got upset and raised her voice, but if ever she did, you knew it was time to stop what you were doing and do something else.

Evangelist Boyd had rules for us to live by, and if you disobeyed those rules, you had to pay the cost. The beliefs that my mother preached about in her sermons and taught in her classes and seminars were the same that she enforced at home. She did not have one personality for church and another for home. Because my whole life and teaching was the same as what went on at church.

As a man of faith, I grew up believing in God and the miracles that could be performed by the people of God. Attending her many Revivals and watching her live the life that she preached was an experience that I now realize was awesome. I lived with someone who stayed in touch with God. No matter how down she was, she still was able to show love and compassion for someone else.

The scripture that says "But the God of all grace, who hath called us unto eternal glory by Christ Jesus, after ye have suffered a while…" would truly apply to my mother, because she truly paid a great price for her place in God (1 Peter 5:10)! I really could not go through the suffering that she went through, but thank God I can say she came through with shining colors. I am not able to put into words what a wonderful and blessed life it has been being the son of Evangelist Mildred Boyd. Because of the life she lived at home and everywhere else, she was able to use her faith to work many miracles in my life. I guess you might say I am a living example of Evangelist Boyd's ministry.

I went out to a nightclub with some friends, and during the course of the evening an argument started between some of my friends and this drunk man we knew. I asked him to leave the table because we didn't want to be bothered with him. He made a remark about my preaching mother. I thought he attempted to hit me in the face, but one of my friends said, "He has a blade." In defense, I struck him with a beer bottle, but he had already cut me in the face. As I was trying to get away, he came towards me, struck me in the back, and opened me up with his blade.

I was rushed to the hospital, but the doctors wouldn't even operate because they said I wouldn't make it through the night.

My aunt and cousin made it to the hospital, and I asked my aunt to call my mother and ask her to come right away. My mother sent word to me that she was praying, and she was on her way. I relaxed then, because I knew that everything would be alright.

By the time my mother packed her suitcases and went from Connecticut to New York, I had lost the battle for my life due to a collapsed lung. When she got to the hospital and was taken to where I was, I had been pronounced dead and was cleaned up and covered over with a sheet. The only thing I remember is her touching me on the shoulder and telling me that everything was going to be alright.

A picture of Otis Boyd. Notice his left nostril. It was the tumor growing in his nose.

The Faith and Life of Mother Boyd

I had a tumor in my nose that made one side of my nose twice as large as the other. Between the ages of 13 and 24, I had four major operations and plastic surgery done to my nose. I almost bled to death on the operating table during two of the operations, and the plastic surgery did not work. I put my faith in the doctors, but my mother kept her faith in God. When I was 24, the tumor became malignant, and the doctor gave me just a few months to live. My nose bled three to four times a week, and the doctors could do nothing to stop it. If they sewed my nose in the spot where it was bleeding, another spot would burst open and bleed.

The last time I went to the hospital, they kept me and decided to try another operation. This time I put my faith with my mother's in God. That last operation was ten years ago, and I no longer have cancer nor any other trouble with my nose.

Most importantly, I am saved and sanctified today because of the things she was able to give me during her lifetime. I could go on and on, but I'll end by saying, "Have faith in God, He can do anything but fail."

Otis Boyd

Mother Boyd's granddaughters at Zion Tabernacle with her pastor Elder Joseph D. Farris.

Revelation 2:10? Mother Boyd made it! "Well done, good and faithful servant!"

A Special Note To You

God is able to heal you now! That's the first fact to believe, regardless of how impossible your case may seem. "The things which are impossible with men are possible with God" (Luke 18:27).

God can do anything now. He is able to heal you now! This is the first step to being healed. Abraham is our example of faith. He was fully persuaded that, what He (God) had promised, He was (is) able to perform (Rom. 4:21). Paul said, "Now unto Him that is able to do exceedingly abundantly above all that we ask or think, according to the power that worketh in us" (Eph. 3:20).

Jesus required this faith of the blind men before He healed them. He asked, "Believe ye that I am able to do this?" They said unto him, "Yea, Lord." Then touched he their eyes, saying, "According to your faith be it unto you" (Mt. 9:28). If God can make the world, the sun, the moon, and the stars, and if God made you and me, then certainly it is just a small thing for Him to heal us when we are sick.

Secondly, God is willing to heal you. The leper questioned Christ's willingness to heal him, saying, "Lord, if thou wilt, thou canst make me clean" (Mt. 8:2). As soon as he said these words, Jesus said, "I will." God's Word, His promises, His convenant, His will, is all the same. He is always willing to fulfill His word, His promise.

He is touched with the feeling of our infirmities (Heb. 3:15). God announces Himself as your healer, thus saying, "I am the Lord that healeth thee," not "I will be," but "I am" (Ps. 103:3). He said, "I am the Lord, I change not" (Mal. 3:6). "He sent his word and healed them" (Ps. 107:20). The remedy is this almighty Word or promise of the Living God.

God Bless,
Mother Boyd

Evang Mildred Boyd

Mother Boyd at Zion Tabernacle, where she was a member.

INDEX

Illness/Affliction	Name of Individual	Results	Page
Osteoporosis	Sis. J. Lucus	Healed	65
Pain	Sis. C. Robinson	Healed	57
Pain	Sis. V. Holmes	Healed	64
Pregnancy	Bro. & Sis. Smith	Healed	77
Pregnancy	Sis. D. Golder	Healed	78
Pregnancy	Sis. F. Watts	Healed	74
Relationship	Sis. B. Foreman	God Provided	98
Sickle Cell Anemia	Sis. B. Shaw	Healed	82
Severe Burns	Bro. C. Humphries	Healed	60
Thyroid	Sis. Plummer	Healed	88
Unknown Sickness	Sis. W. Harrison	Healed	84

Other Books from Just Word Publishing

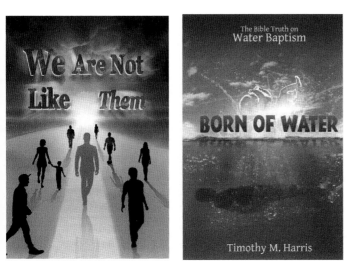

BORN OF
SPIRIT
(Coming Soon)

MOFAITH
(Coming Soon)